Gifts From the Earth

Contents

Rocks 4
Marble 6
Granite 8
Gold 10
Silver 12
Salt 14
Chalk 16

Susan Ring

We get many gifts
from the earth.

We dig for these gifts.

Rocks are gifts from the earth.

Some rocks are used for jewelry.

Marble Quarry

Marble is a gift from the earth.

Lincoln Memorial

Marble is used for statues and buildings.

Granite is a gift from the earth.

Granite is used for buildings.

Gold Nugget

Gold is a gift from the earth.

Egyptian Mask

Gold is used to make things.

Silver Crystals

Silver is a gift from the earth.

Silver is used to make things.

Salt Mine

Salt is a gift from the earth.
Salt is used for cooking.

Salt Spreader

Salt is also used to melt snow.

Have you ever used chalk?
Chalk is a gift
from the earth, too.